Sincerely,

Freda Bair

Frieda Bair

FEATHER IN THE WIND

Dorrance & Company • *Philadelphia*

ISBN 0-8059-2183-4
Printed in the United States of America

To
Lisa Ann
Gayle Lynne
Jenna Lee
and
all the young at heart

CONTENTS

FEATHER IN THE WIND

KALEIDOSCOPE

Life is a candid camera recording
  Day by day the many and varied happenings
That somehow come one's way;
  Each exposure is uniquely different
With flashbacks from time to time,
  As dreams and untold memories
Manage to come to mind.
  There is romance filled with laughter.
There is tragedy and there are tears.
  The film may be short or it may be long,
Depending upon one's years;
  But what is developed becomes a print
Most fascinating to see, depending on a pose
  Taken of you or me.

LIFE

Who can say exactly what life is all about,
Except the fact that we are here
And there is no other route to where
Day ends and night descends?
But this we know, and it is so,
That as we journey here, there's much
To do and feel and see in this life's mystery.
There may be more questions than answers,
There may be more tears than smiles,
With so little time for laughter
And less time for what comes after
The music stops;
But this life is still worth living
If one takes the time for giving
What matters most of this and that,
With less concern for self and hate.

SEARCH

Man is born with a questing mind,
  And endless is the search
To know the why and wherefore
  Of whatever may exist.
He probes the earth and scans the skies;
  He flits across the sea
In the hope of gaining knowledge new
  Of unknown things that be.
One lifetime is much too short
  To all but scratch the surface,
But each, by unearthing what he can,
  Enrichment he will lend,
With added meaning to hiddenness
  And light on what is penned.

YESTERDAY

Today I say and it is so, who writes tomorrow
  Will not know how stern the struggle
    Here below.
Life's ending only shows the glow of embers
    Consumed in joy or woe,
And who can tell when ashes fell, what
    Tinder went into the strife
Of this or that frail feeble life?
Those close at hand may think it's true
That they can speak for me or you,
  But only God can paint the whole
With colors where they ought to be,
  And only He, not you or me,
Reveals what happened secretly.

CREATION

When God made man, He put a spark
  Of creativity into his heart,
With a plan that each in his own way
  Might help create a bright new day.
The names are many, to express this gift,
  And the degree of skill most varied;
But although oft dormant, delayed or blocked,
  The gift is there while life exists.
To paint, to write, to sew or sing,
  All these, and more, are but the thing
To implement a dream: This urge to extend
  The self beyond mere existence to
The joy of being.

Oh, it would seem a foolish jest
  If man would fail to do his best
In creating something from his skill,
  Unique, divinely prompted, and released
To fill a need to do the very thing
  That he alone can ultimately bring
As an offering of a fruitful life.

EMERGENCE

Some living things are eager to mature,
Like snowdrops in bloom beneath a blanket white,
Where joyously they stretch toward sun and rain,
And prematurely burst the bonds of earth again.
Too soon the time when these are gone,
Since they can't afford to linger long.
But other growing things are destined to remain
More leisurely within the nest, to rest upon
The breast, and wait the thrust that ends
Their lethargy. These, like the oak, need
Time to grow and build within their frame
The strength to stand life's strain, and so . . .
Unhurried they remain late bloomers.

PRIMER

Stark, against the sky, lone and abandoned,
Stands the one-room school,
With wide plank floor and strong oak door,
Potbellied stove in use no more.
Replaced, we boast a spacious span
Encased in brick, with carpets thick,
Plus air conditioning and intercom,
Cushioned seats in the auditorium,
And revolving desks for Sue and Tom.
The teachers, too, are a special breed,
Trained to meet each pupil's need.
But, alas and alack, in the modern school
There remains no room for the Golden Rule.

INTERLUDE

For a time we walked along the way,
  Just you and I together;
Your smile was bright and step so light,
  And perfect was the weather,
As I prayed the days would always be
  So right for us together;
But fate had planned it otherwise,
  And clouds transformed the weather.
The sky grew dark, with a sudden flash;
  The rain poured on us together.
Confused and stunned, we dashed about
  In search of a dry sheltered spot,
But all we found at wild storm's end
  Was just a drenched fair-weather friend
  And parting was forever.

AN OFFERING

Love, joy, and peace—these three
  Were meant to be shared by you and me:
To love, not as the selfish do,
  Who blind with chain each little claim,
But freely give and take life's gift.
  No room remains for hoarded hurts
Or clutched fears that never know
  The love found in forgiving.

Joy shouts no worldly bliss, but this:
  A bursting forth of self in vibrant glow
To all who know and understand, a heaven within,
  The joy that comes from giving.

Peace, that rare pearl of so great price,
  Found chiefly through much sacrifice
    Of what life holds so dear;
This to give that others, too, may live,
  And thus to find some cause for being.

CURIOSITY

Windows are the eyes of home,
  Filled with meaning for you and me;
They tell of wealth, or loss of hope,
  Or just simple poverty.
Some shine with perfect curtains,
  Others flash a well-worn blind,
And at times, a face peers from the frame
  Seen by someone passing by
Long enough to catch a smile, a tear,
  Or even hear a sigh.
I often try to read the tale
  That windows tell to me,
And find it much more interesting
  Than other imagery;
For when my own cares weigh me down,
  From experience, I have learned
To look around to a window found
  To arouse curiosity,
Because when I do, I always come
  To this very sure conclusion:
That some chapter in another's life
  Helps to dispel my own delusion.

CONTOUR

Ours is the body-conscious age,
  A time for keeping spry,
When young and old their years defy
  And keep wrestling till they die.
Some choose the sports and swat a ball;
  Still others prefer swimming,
And many jog for miles and miles,
  Keeping count of who is winning.
Gregarious folks will join a class
  Of meditation, yoga, or the spa,
While others hunt a fallen log, some
  Firewood to saw.
More practical souls will hoe and sweat
  And manage to keep trim by planting seeds
And hoping for some produce to bring in.

Thus, endless are the ways that man
  Strives to keep from growing old,
As he works and plays until the day when
  Exercise is vain, and he must settle
For a walk on days it does not rain.

Although Father Time may grant a reprieve
  To faithful activists, he is the victor in the end,
For when all is said and done, no one has ever yet devised
  A way to keep the body forever young.

EMBRYO

Leafless trees in patience waiting
  For the pulse of life to stir and beat
Once again within each heart, free and warm,
  Full and sweet.
How painlessly each opening bud,
  Stretching blade of grass, and peeping bulb
Reaches out and up, to yawn and greet another dawn,
  To smile awhile, then droop and sleep,
And find retreat in slumber sweet at season's eve.

These things life cannot take from me,
  Which changeless as the seasons are,
So safe from sun and blasts that blow,
  Things that stay green and ever new;
Which blossom forth from time to time and
  In original lustre shine . . .
These precious memories of mine!

LESSER LIGHTS

There are the great and glorious lights
  Which dance before one's eyes:
The sun, the moon, and nearby stars,
  Providing wonder and surprise;
But there are also lesser lights, abundant
  In the sky, wee sparks that glow
So faithfully in the mantle known as night.
  It is the distance that makes some seem
Both dim and without worth, but they are there
  To enhance the whole and add meaning
To the earth.
  If size and proximity mattered most
In a boundless galaxy, we would be compelled
  To forget lesser lights which form
The Milky Way.

WORDS

Words can hurt and words can heal;
Words express just how we feel.
Hate-filled words can only bring
An aching heart, and leave a sting
That lasts for years.
Loving words can ease a pain
And clear the sky of clouds and rain.
Words are like magic, with power to spell
A life of heaven or a life of hell.
So ponder well the kindly word,
And leave unsaid what brings regret,
For anger prompts the tongue to speak
What later proves hard to forget;
And those who quell the bitter word
Are among the blessed and gladly heard.

PASSING THOUGHTS

Traveling a monotonous highway
  Can be something of a bore
Unless one seeks out hidden things
  To sometimes puzzle o'er,
And see in passing vehicles
  A specific mystery.
First, a gay and costly car zips by,
  Arousing admiration,
Followed by a beat-up truck loaded
  With junk beyond recognition;
Next, moving cautiously on its way
  Is a camper filled with kids,
A dog, and some kittens, too.
  As each travels in a different world
With a story so unique that one wishes
  It were possible to stop and hear each tale;
But since it is not sensible on a highway
  Built for speed, one can only relax
With eyes on the road, and construct a plot
  To meet the need of the people
    Speeding by.

CAPSTONE

Poetry is more than rhyme or metered line
And words sublime;
It is the mind and soul's expression
Of joy or pain, intended to proclaim
What may be deeply felt or seen as a dream
Come to life and flashed upon a screen.

Poetry is silence made articulate,
Like thunder on a quiet day,
Or a rainbow at storm's ending.
What's left unsaid speaks softly
Between the lines or hovers like an
Angel's wing, to whisper soft caresses.

The poet's soul is a restless thing:
It pants for breath on mountain peaks
Or gasps in the valley of despair,
As it flits and soars like thistledown
Or rolls like tumbleweed, as it wrestles
With verbiage frail to snare the comet's tail.

SEASONING

Summer grows tired and waits for the call
To make a quick exit in welcome of Fall,
For balmy days are about to end,
As October tips green with a startling
Blend of yellow and red, and glorifies life
Before striking it dead with fingers so sharp,
And winds that blow shrill like the strings of a harp.

When Fall, too, is gone, Mother Earth grows old
As she sheds her garment of crimson and gold,
And greedily clutches her blanket of white
To warm her cold frame far into the night;
And thus she will doze, and dream for a while,
Until spring tiptoes in with a warm, winning smile
To announce once again that sleeping must end,
And made room for change in the garb of a friend.

RESPONDABILITY

Neurosis, psychosis, complexes and *fixation*
  Are terms we encounter day after day.
In fact, they've swept the nation.
  We observe our friends and discover signs
Of this or that obsession, and wonder if they
  Are quite mature, or merely keeping one guessin'
About what type of mental quirk they flaunt
  Before one's eyes, but it could be that
They are just naive, and observers are not wise.
  Superior or inferior, laymen seldom can decide
Exactly who is stable, confused, or otherwise;
  And so it's best to recognize that when a personality
With a certain peculiarity or unusual individuality
  Confronts one with a "Hi!" it's normal not
To raise a brow or seriously question why.

TRIBUTE TO A FRIEND

If only all could have a friend
  In whom he could confide,
Someone, no matter what the score,
  Who would understand, not chide;
But friends like that are hard to find,
  And seldom found, 'tis true,
For almost everyone we know avoids us
  When we're blue and only seeks
Us out again when winds have ceased to blow.
  God, give us friends who stick close by
Regardless of the weather, and love us
  In our every mood, just glad to
    Be together.
For there are summer friends and "pop-in" friends
  And a few for a lifetime long,
But the friends who always mean the most
  Are around when things go wrong.

ANALYSIS

At heart, we are so much the same,
That it helps one to absolve from blame,
His brother.
We are like children, despite our age,
And hide from fears to act the sage;
Yet underneath that stoic look,
We read each other like a book
When we see a flicker of alarm
At the dread of some impending harm,
That man is plotting secretly.
No one has earned a conscience free,
Until he lives in harmony
With God and man and makes
A habit of integrity.

THANK GOD

There is so much to thank God for,
  In spite of pain and sorrow,
Especially for the hope that brings
  A promising tomorrow.
There is so much to thank God for
  When we take the time to see
The beauty which surrounds us
  In such great variety.
The thrill of summer, spring, and fall,
  And winter's peace, so still, and all
The wonder of this fleeting life,
  Beyond the realm of hurt and strife.
One's spirit cannot linger long on
  What there is that seems so wrong
When a rainbow arches in the sky or
  A cardinal swiftly flashes by
To lift the thoughts to God on high
  In goodness felt, in loved ones near,
In things to do, in a day that's new;
  All this and more we thank God for!

HOLY HARMONY

The manger scene is a family scene,
  Featuring father, mother, and babe;
The setting is spare, but love is there,
  A glorious combination,
The best of God's creation.

From far and near, love draws those dear
  At Christmastime.
There is no fear when God is near.
  For Herod is dead; Christ reigns instead.

Above earth's din, the angels sing,
  Filling the air with a sweet refrain,
Stilling man's striving for acclaim
  As love is born each Christmas morn.

Old wounds are healed at Christmastime,
  Each cross becomes a star,
As love and joy and hope renew
  Man's weakening faith and lift his soul
To where celestial encounter provides
  The Christmas feast at the Savior's feet.

HOME

A bride's house is her castle, so I'm told,
Which she enters with hopes of shining gold,
And flits from room to room, where beams
Of sunshine furnish all with happy dreams.

As wife, the scene may shift a bit:
His cozy chair and slippers seem to fit
The picture well, for she knows
That love has come to dwell.

A mother now, with baby's cries and all
The other changes in the cottage small,
Where time and things accumulate to add a touch,
And growing, mean so very much:
A bronzed shoe rests upon the shelf
Beside a pale blue slipper from the past
And later on, to fill a vacant place,
A spotted vase for Mother's Day.
And so each year, a thing or two is placed
To gather dust and stir a memory;
Some sad, some gay, but each in a special way
A bridge from earth to heaven, so they say.

RESPONSE

A piteous sight on a wintry day,
Is watching a sparrow gently sway
On the bar of an empty feeder,
While snug and warm, and amply fed,
I peer through the window and shake my head,
And wish for a better way instead
Of wading through snow up to my knees,
Plus facing a bitter, chilling breeze
To restock the larder from end to end
With a variety of seeds for my feathered friend.
But since there seems no other way
To feed the birds that pass each day,
I grab a bag of multiple seeds,
And forge a track through the snow-covered weeds
To satisfy for another day what every living
Creature needs.

UNFULFILLED

It's hard to wait for what you want
  And watch the years go by
Without the longed-for goal in sight
  And hopes no longer high.

It's hard to wait and watch your dreams
  Fade slowly out of reach
And know that the time may never come
  When plans will no longer
Lie untouched like pebbles on the beach.

It's hard to kiss the years good-bye
  And feel no longer young,
Yet still to wish for one small success
  Before the setting sun.

LONGING

The wistfulness of childlessness is a touching sight to see,
With shattered hopes and dreams of things that never came to be,
The empty arms, and heart so full of love for a child so wee,
And yet some folks are envious of what they chance to see.

How still the days and nights in homes without a babe or two,
How missing are the toys and clutter in a house so very new!
How can one compensate for things that money buys
Until one looks with pity into another's eyes?

Would you trade the growing, happy days one knows with girls
And boys, and all the little hurts and tears that happen
Along the way, for the loneliness in growing old
With memories never known—the tiny hand, the empty nest—
Like swallows that have flown?

So save your envy, my friends so dear, and cast a second
Glance upon the ones so free in life who never had a chance
To hold life's very special gift and all that it entails,
And breathe a prayer and thank the Lord for snails and long
Pigtails.

WINGS

Above and round about in busy spring,
Winged things fly;
They have a destiny to fulfill
And nature will not wait for nests
Long overdue, nor rest through summer's heat,
For little ones must learn to fly and search
For food before spring comes again.
Wings were meant to flutter, hover, soar
And finally drop to fan the wind and rain
No more. For final flight is evermore.

MIGRANTS

My feathered, southbound friends are back
  To briefly say, "hello"
And pause just long enough to rest
  And snatch a crumb or two,
While they check to see if I'm around
  To welcome their brief flight
Before they chirp a swift farewell
  And vanish with the night.
Nature's time clock seems to set the pace
  For whatever lives and grows,
As each responds according to
  The seasonal wind that blows.

HOROSCOPE

Old planet Earth must rue the day
When humankind invented a way
To increase extermination by vain exploitation.
The urge to kill, not just for food
But for vanity and a price, to rip the feathers
And the hide from fowl and beast, a gory share
Of plumage and pelts to proudly wear
In fashion's latest craze.
From age to age, with increased greed,
He stripped the valleys of grass and seed
As mountains shook and streams ran wild,
But all in vain, for Earth's wayward child
Still chose to plunder, rape, and kill,
And use whatever newfound skill
To pollute the waters, field, and air
And poison whatever life was there,
Until at last he stands alone,
Stripped of glory, fame, and power
Realizing at last, as he hears Earth groan,
That this indeed is the final hour.

CHALLENGE

This is a fresh new day, with another chance
To do the things that were left undone,
To sing the song waiting to be sung,
To make amends and to chart a course
That will be for the better, not the worse.
But be that as it may, there still is time
To pray to realize a way to solve
Each firm resolve, or a bit of what's amiss.
And so with the help of God to guide the way,
One welcomes this, and each new day,
Forgetting what has gone before,
And as though standing before an open door, to
Pass through without a backward look,
Lest like Lot's wife, one fails to see
The distant hills and what can be.

BROKEN REED

How does one feel when a loved one dies?
No numbness can compare or tears repair
The shattered self.
Emptiness moves in, and stillness, too,
As softly love whispers, "I care, and
Have come to share your loneliness."

Why must one weep when a loved one dies?
Is it because the pain of parting cries
For hope to see beyond what is, to what
Must be, or does remembering all that
Went before, and is no more, bring tears?

The sun has set and day is gone,
And yet tomorrow still will come
To bless and heal, as shadows of the
Past live on.

PHILOSOPHY

I watched the birds at feeding time,
And it was good to see how well
They managed to get on.
The small ones waited patiently
Until the larger ones were fed,
Then took their place accordingly
And ate remaining bread.
They did not need as much to live
As I was wont to think, but only
To be left alone with room enough
To fly, to build a nest, and teach
Their young some bird philosophy.

LATE TRAVELER

Life more cruel than death can be
For those with eyes that do not see,
For all who grope in blind despair
And know not how to seek, or where,
For purpose in life's dull routine.
And so I cannot weep for those
Who peacefully rest in last repose,
Who, cut off early in their prime,
Have missed so much of mire and grime,
Yet found life sweet and spread their wings
And bid farewell while the heart still sings.
These surely are prepared for things
Which heaven reserves for those with wings.
But have pity, Lord, on all who wait
And finally leave when it is late;
For burdened surely are their backs
With shattered dreams and heavy sacks
Of worthless gems no longer bright.
Lord, grant a final bit of grace
To all who linger on the way,
Who cannot go, yet would not stay
If God had planned an earlier day
To end the sojourn here on earth.

MOODS

Moods, like the weather, change from day to day;
Often we are inclined to fret,
Less often to rejoice, depending on the choice
Of what we do or say.
Events determine so very much of
How we chance to feel; for some
Bring sunshine, others rain,
And so uplift or cast a gloom
On the spirit of the day.
Life has its share of rainy times,
And sunny times, 'tis true;
But how our mood reflects each change
Depends on me and you.

GHETTO

Spring:

Cold, bleak, and oh so noisy:
The voice of vendors shouting, "Cabbage!"
The rattle of garbage cans tossed from trucks.
Absent, oh so absent:
Bird song and hyacinth, but everpresent, hope.

Summer:

Hot and feverish, and oh so humid.
Missing from the scene: Cool pools and
Shaded lawns, breeze-swept trees, but hope lingering.

Fall:

Dust and smell of summer's end:
No painted leaves or autumn glow,
Just whiffs of smoke from chimneys low,
And listless hope.

Winter:

Black snow and smog and oh so cold:
Bitterness and tears. Dead hope.

DUALITY

Flesh and blood would seem to be
In conflict with spirituality;
For spirit clashes swords with earth,
And man decides what each is worth.
All pay the price of fame and wealth,
When it interferes with health;
Or worse than that, he sells his soul,
Like Faust, who bargained for a toll.
But for him who heeds the spirit's call,
Truth must come first, and claim his all.
With open eyes, each takes his task
From day to day, nor stops to ask
The price, or what rewards will be
Expected now or eternally.
Content to work and trust and pray,
The righteous walk the broad highway.

EASTER SONG

We praise our Christ, God's deathless Son,
  Forever throned, Eternal One!
Through ages past and years to come,
  We pray indeed, "Thy will be done!"

"Man cannot live by bread alone,"
  Thy word sustains and leads us home,
And ever binds us, one and all,
  To Thy great love when we
    Hear Thy call.

No black today can dim the hope
  Of better days to be,
No setting sun but speaks of dawn,
  No shattered dream but inspires song,
And for all with steadfast faith in God
  No night is long.

REVEILLE

Rainbow colors blaze once more
Across our land, from shore to shore,
As graves are decked in every hue,
Symbolic of remembrance true.
Fingers fumble pots of clay, as moistened
With tears are blossoms gay;
Varied as thumbprints are memories this day.
Row on row, flags briskly blow
In tribute to the ones we know,
Who gave half-lived lives that we might live.
Marchers, like puppets, parade the street,
To the rhythm of a great heartbeat,
And pause where the dead and living meet,
To mark once more the passing from the scene
Of those who lie beneath the green.
Though names may be fading fast from view,
These still rank high among the few
Who knew what war was all about.
While death may claim this special day,
So does life, in reflection sweet,
Where here at the crossing, both now meet,
And life alone knows no defeat.

SERIOUSLY

The war is over, so they say,
  And hopefully peace has come to stay;
But doubt and hate still linger on,
  And victory did not bring a song
Because so many thought it wrong
  To fight and kill on distant shores,
While at home we had our private wars.

The war is over, so they say,
  But faith is lacking on all sides,
  As preparations still go on to keep the peace;
So arms continue to increase, just in case
  Some nation fails to know its place,
And tries again to win the race
  By methods frowned upon.

It is by trusting that we rise or fall,
  And not by some dividing wall
That keeps some in and others out.
  The time has come to turn about,
Lest lacking one more victory,
  Mankind will ever cease to be.

GRATITUDE

Thank God I had your hand to hold,
  Your arms to shield me from the cold,
Your heart to understand and know
  How weak I am when cruel winds blow.

Thank God you came before despair
  Had darkened all the sky so fair;
You brought fresh hope to spur me on
  When life and light were almost gone.

Thank God you brought me through the night,
  And soothed the pain and stilled the fright,
And loosed the bonds to set me free
  To chart my course for days to be.

TO YOU

Dear friend, who only sees the good
  And brings out all the best in me,
To you I owe the best in life,
  So free from evil and from strife.
Because in love you bore my cross,
  That I might know less pain and loss.
God's richest gift to me, it seems,
  And one beyond my fondest dreams,
Is in having a friend so tried and true.
  May I someday be a friend like you!

DIRECTION

Old head on shoulders young,
Sad-eyed, no time for sun and play;
Young head on shoulders old,
Eyes gay, intent on play at late day.
Old too soon, or young too late,
Nature denied, has sighed and cried
At such sorry fate
That seeks fulfillment in the end.
There is a season, time, and place
For all that live in earth's domain,
And stretch upward toward the sun;
Blighted are those that contrarily run.

THE TWELVE

They found Him not in pillared halls
  Nor sanctuary grand,
But bending o'er a prostrate form,
  And reaching out a hand
To one laid low on life's highway
  And left alone to die.
'Twas there they saw the God of love,
  So free from pride and scorn,
As He knelt beside the helpless one,
  Afflicted and forlorn.
He placed his hand upon his brow,
  To his eager lips a cup,
And drew from His pouch a crust of bread,
  And then He raised him up.
So the seekers of the "Lord of Life"
  Turned from the vaulted dome
To walk with Him the chosen path,
  Where the broken lie and moan.

PREPARATION

Lent is a time for serious thought,
  A time of meditation;
It is a time to fast and pray,
  A time for contemplation.
Lent is a time to look within,
  A time of realization
Of just what means the most in life,
  A time of revelation.
So Lent becomes a holy time,
  A time of preparation
For all the joy that Easter brings,
  A time of resurrection.

MYSTERY

If we knew all there was to know,
Then search would end in the world below;
But beyond and above what we see and feel
Is the vast unknown, which is also real.
The things of spirit know no tomb;
They also exist and have a home
In the heart of God, who planned it so,
That we in time may come to know
That He is God and rules the earth
In spite of how man measures worth.
Explosive joy at Easter time
Still lifts the spirit to heights sublime.
No grave can hold Christ's mighty passion,
No height nor depth keep Him confined.
Life and love can know no boundary;
Only hate and fear can bind.
Hope will never cease to be
While so much of living is mystery.

PARADOX

Our work, it seems, is born with us;
  But be that as it may,
Each one possesses a talent
  To use in a special way;
If all were equipped with identical skills,
  To carry out God's will,
The world would be a sorry mess
  For lack of a special skill.
There are dreamers and there are doers
  In this wide world of ours;
As the dreamers draft the blueprints
  While the doers construct a mall
To put the dreams where all can see,
  A reality grand and tall.
The thought, the word, the deeds are tools
  To be used or cast aside;
But what matters most is meeting a need
  With dignity and with pride.
So although you differ some from me
  And I from you, 'tis true,
That it makes the things we do more fun,
  Like a trophy newly won.

WINTER

Nude trees stand stark against the sky,
  Stripped bare of green and gold,
    Cold, yet bold.
Erect, and unashamed, as on parade,
  With nothing now to give
    Of beauty, or of shade,
Except the hidden gift no eye can see:
  The promise of spring
    And maturity.
This is the dormant time when life
    Stands still,
The waiting time until the thrill
    And warmth of spring
Will thaw the frozen heart
    And bid life sing.

ECSTASY

For many of us the song's the same:
  We rejoice to see snowflakes again,
Since a new, fresh beauty has come our way
  To lift the heart on a winter's day.
The thrill of cold shadows on the snow,
  And the sound of crunching ice below
Hurried feet as prismatic icicles,
  Dazzling bright, are pure magic to the sight.
Tall pines weighed down with mantle white
  Fill passers-by with delight at such loveliness
Created for you and me,
  And reflectingly we see how beautiful
This world can be.

INSIGHT

When motives are the very best
  And love is in the giving,
The heart responds as "deep to deep"
  As life becomes worth living.
But if for reasons hid from view,
  The giver witholds love,
Then the gift is vain and counts
  For naught in the record kept above.
But when duty ends and love begins,
  There comes a special joy,
Known only to the one who feels
  Like a happy girl or boy.

SUNDOWN

I awoke to find not dawn, but dusk,
  When suddenly I felt old.
What nightmare robbed me of the years,
  Like a story still untold?
What fleeting forms had fled this life,
  What fancied joys and futile strife
Have slipped away to God knows where,
  And left me standing lone and bare
Like an empty tree, sans fruit and leaf,
  Gnarled and old?

Better to have slept on, remembering not
  The fleeting kiss of a tiny tot,
Or a cherished love and realized dream
  Than to awake with lingering years
Devoid of promise, yet so few in which
  To live and laugh and do
The things still left for me and you.

ALMANAC

Each age, like a season, has a beauty of its own,
From the wee seed in springtime to the harvest full-blown.
The tender years of childhood overflow with song,
While youth seeks adventure to help things along.
The mellow years behold life with a tolerant eye,
To better enjoy the wherefore and the why.
But old age reflects on days gone by,
And chuckles o'er memories that will not die.
Thus each age, like the seasons, has its good times and bad,
With the small hurts of childhood and scars of youth,
And middle years, too, have their story of woe.
But who can deny that the pain and the hurt
Were all part of growing, as God planned it so,
Mid trial and temptation to muse and to sigh,
Aware all along that there comes a time we must die.

HATS OFF!

Thoughts are long and words are few
In expressing one's point of view
Now that the war is over.
Still stunned from years of strife
And hate, it's difficult to relate
To an uneasy peace.

But this we know, be it friend or foe,
Our hearts go out to the POW,
Who bore the weight of cruel fate,
And survived once more to set foot
On his beloved home shore.

Hats off to all who lived and died
To speed the day when the world will say,
"No more, no more, this thing called war!"

MOTHER'S DAY

Tall sons and daughters fair,
Scattered here and there,
Reflect some home and mother's care.
But sad the ones who, far from home,
And perfectly content to roam,
Seldom take the time to think
Of those who gave them life.
Cold walls surround the thoughtless ones
Who lack the warmth of comforting,
And still in need of mothering.
Now once a year on Mother's Day,
There comes the urge to pause and pray
Or say a loving word or two,
Remembering the one who had some
Time for mothering.

CENTELEBRATION

Written for the hundredth anniversary of the village of East Aurora, New York, 1974.

This is the time to celebrate one hundred years of growing,
A time to recollect the past and highlight that worth knowing.
It is a season of thankfulness for visions realized,
And gratitude to those who mapped the course
For better or for worse.
There were the Adamses, Godfreys, Persons, Peeks, and Hubbards,
Pioneers, to mention but a few.
They, too, had their good days and their bad, with happy days
And sad, yet valued what they had.
Now it is ours to celebrate their courage and their worth,
And find the strength to carry on in footprints of the past
With prayer and faith that good will last
To bless the coming years, that others, too, may celebrate
Our challenging golden years.

SUBSTANCE

Strong souls develop like the oak
  And mellow with the years;
They bend not with each passing breeze,
  Nor bow to all the other trees.
Deep-rooted they stand and stretch their limbs,
  A nesting place for birds and food for friends
In winter long, and shade for man ere day be gone.
  What more than rest and food and love
Can one soul to another give?
  God bless the ones who oaklike live,
Stand firm and grow, but mostly give!

SOLITARY JOURNEY

The road each travels is a lonesome path
Beset with briars and this and that
To stay the step and cause alarm.
One knows how useful one may be in some small scheme;
Another warms himself in a bright smile
And stays a while.
Each takes what others give, save tears and toil,
And seldom stays to pray when skies are gray.
The cross is still a solitary proposition,
And all must bear its weight alone,
For the road is long and we are solitary pilgrims.

SILVER SAINT

No flowing robes, no halo bright,
Nothing to delight the sight
Of those who gaze on her.
Wrinkled brow gives grace somehow
To hair fresh streaked with gray.
Her hands so capable and strong
Are quick to find and right a wrong,
And always in her heart, a song,
A song that sings through twinkling eyes,
A song of courage that never dies;
And so she is both sweet and wise,
Never quite able to disguise a smile.
We seldom think of her as good
Or better in a special way;
It is enough that she always stood
In readiness to fill our day
With gladness, or perhaps a tear
And tender touch to quell a fear.
She lives today in such a way
That all who know her want to say
That she's a saint, but she knows
Quite well that she's only quaint
And chooses to be "Gram."

JANE DOE

I know Jane Doe, for she lives next door to me.
Look through my window and see what you can see:
An average home, six rooms at best, and painted white,
And shubbery, plus a garden plot, well planned,
Three husky children and a dog of black,
A busy mother in and out, well tanned.
This is her castle and her life and love.

Oh, yes, John Doe—his car just stopped in front;
He bangs the door of his chariot bright,
Dressed in a pinstripe suit, of course,
For he is one of the office force.
He kisses his wife and children three,
And pats the dog—a king is he.
His dinner waits and the newspaper, too,
And a list of little jobs to do.
And so it goes from day to day,
And who of us can ever say that it should
Be another way, since it is they who set the pace
With others like them in this place?
Suburban life is no rat race.

RUMMAGE SALE

Kind folks have gathered things
  Which they no longer want,
That others may find what they need
  To fill an empty spot.
It is great fun to see how much
  That can be cast aside by those
No longer poor, and what it means
  To longing souls to find some beauty there.
A few things are marred and need repair,
  But others are like new.
And as I pass, I add my bit in sorrow
  And despair—just one poor bruised
And broken heart—and pray that you'll
  Find it there.

TOMORROW

The burdens of today are quite enough to bear
  Without thoughts of past regrets
    Or future pain and fear.
If on can only do his best on this and every day
  And trust and pray that God knows best
    For each along the way,
How many anxious moments we'd miss,
  How much more strength for good,
By simply living each today as trusting
    Children should.
Life has its ups and downs, 'tis true,
  But none are meant to stay.
So a happier tomorrow must follow each today,
  When we lift our heart and chin, my friend,
And struggle one day more, for it just may be
  That opportunity will come knocking
    On one's door.